MW00900436

DETROIT

TRAVEL GUIDE

2023

Discover The Soul Of The Midwest: A
Detroit Travel Guide. What to See, Do, and
Eat in the City

NICOLAS MENDEZ

TABLE OF CONTENTS

INTRODUCTION

The "**Detroit Travel Guide 2023**," your ticket to an exciting adventure through the Motor City, is here to welcome you. Detroit, a city renowned for its deep cultural past, dynamic character, and one-of-a-kind charm, entices visitors with a wide range of activities.

Explore the fascinating mix of history and innovation that characterizes Detroit today by using this tour. Explore the Motown music's history, stroll through neighborhoods brimming with art, and indulge in Detroit's expanding culinary scene. There is something for every tourist, from the spectacular architecture of Downtown to the natural haven of Belle Isle.

Detroit offers something for everyone, whether you're a history buff, a music fan, a gourmet, or an explorer. To ensure that your time in Detroit is as productive as possible, we have compiled crucial data, insider knowledge, and local knowledge. So buckle on as we go off in 2023 to discover the spirit of this legendary American metropolis.

Welcome to Detroit

Welcome to Detroit, a thriving and dynamic city with a strong sense of invention and creativity. As soon as you walk into the busy streets of Motor City, you start a trip rich in history, culture, and a special fusion of traditional enchantment and contemporary rejuvenation.

About this Guide

You may count on our thorough "**Detroit Travel Guide 2023**" as your reliable travel companion. Whether you're here for a weekend break or a longer exploration, it's made to make the most of your stay.

Getting to Know Detroit

Culture and History

To appreciate Detroit, one must understand its past, which is a patchwork of victories and setbacks. Start your adventure by learning about Detroit's fascinating history, from its Native American beginnings to its significance as the city that gave birth to Motown music. To learn more about the history of the city, visit institutions like the Charles H. Wright Museum of African American History and the Detroit Historical Museum.

The city has a vibrant cultural scene as well. With renowned organizations like the Detroit Institute of Arts displaying an astounding collection of artwork from all eras and cultures, Detroit is home to a flourishing arts scene. To fully experience Detroit's creative heritage, go to a concert by the Detroit Symphony Orchestra or a live play at one of the city's historic theaters.

Neighborhoods

Each of Detroit's different neighborhoods has a distinct tale to tell, much like the many chapters in a gripping book. With recognizable buildings, Campus Martius Park, and a developing culinary scene, the downtown region is a hive of activity. Discover Greektown to experience the thriving nightlife and delectable Mediterranean food.

The Cultural Center and Midtown are pillars of creativity, learning, and innovation. Take a stroll around the Detroit Science Center or stop by the Cultural Center Historic District to see the sculptures and paintings. Corktown and Eastern Market nearby provide a sample of the regional cuisine of Detroit. The biggest public market in the country is located in Eastern Market, and Corktown's ancient streets are lined with quaint restaurants and breweries.

For a peaceful haven, go to Belle Isle Park, a treasure in the Detroit River. The beautiful gardens, aquarium, and breathtaking views of the metropolitan skyline are all features of this island haven. It's the ideal location for a relaxing afternoon picnic or a beautiful riverside bike ride.

Local Cuisine

Detroit's varied population and immigrant cultures have left their culinary mark on the city, creating a wonderful blend of tastes. Detroit-style pizza, the city's national cuisine, must be sampled while there. It's a delectable experience you won't soon forget, distinguished by its square form, thick, crispy crust, and toppings that go all the way to the edges.

The city provides a wide variety of gastronomic delicacies in addition to pizza. Taquerias in Mexicantown provide mouthwatering tacos and tasty salsas, so explore the neighborhood for true Mexican food. Try traditional soul cuisine dishes like fried chicken and collard greens at neighborhood hotspots in the old areas.

The breweries in Detroit are a delight if you like craft beer. With breweries like Founders and Atwater Brewery providing a broad variety of beers to fit every palette, the craft beer sector has grown in recent years.

Food trucks in Detroit are also a must-try since they provide a variety of international cuisines. These mobile kitchens bring culinary innovation to the streets, serving anything from gourmet burgers to tacos with Korean BBQ.

Your key to discovering Detroit's fascinating diversity is this guide. With it in your possession, you're prepared to explore the historical sites, exciting neighborhoods, and delectable food that distinguish Detroit as a unique travel destination. So buckle up, and get ready to go through the Motor City's historic center on an amazing excursion.

PLANNING YOUR TRIP

Making sure your vacation to Detroit is memorable and pleasurable begins with careful planning. To make the most of your trip to the Motor City, follow the instructions in this section.

When to Visit

The attraction of Detroit never fades, but the time of year you come may have a big influence on how you feel.

Seasons and Weather

All four of the seasons are fully experienced in Detroit, giving each a different perspective on the city.

Spring (March–May): Detroit has a rejuvenating spring. In Belle Isle Park, cherry blossoms bloom, bringing vitality to the city's gardens. It's the perfect time of year for outdoor exploring because of the pleasant weather.

Summer (June–August): The summer season is warm and energetic, with a variety of outdoor festivals, concerts, and activities. The city's many parks are ideal for picnics and strolls, and the Detroit Riverfront is bustling with events.

Autumn (September to November): Detroit's fall foliage is breathtaking. A magnificent background for touring the city's neighborhoods and parks is provided by the crisp air and vibrant leaves. Indulge in locally produced vegetables at farmers' markets as it's harvest season.

Winter in Detroit is a white paradise (December to February). As the weather decreases, the festive mood intensifies. A warm environment is produced by Campus Martius Park's ice skating and the holiday decorations across the city. If you like winter activities, the surrounding ski resorts provide exhilarating excursions.

Festivals and Special Events

The many annual festivals and special events held in Detroit give your trip additional flare.

Movement Electronic Music Festival (Memorial Day Weekend): Detroit, sometimes referred to as **"Techno City,"** is where techno music first emerged. Top DJs and electronic musicians perform at this event, which attracts music lovers from all over the globe.

The world-famous **North American International Car Show**, which takes place in January, is a must-attend event for car aficionados to see the newest developments. It is an example of cutting-edge design and technology.

Enjoy free jazz concerts by regional and international performers at the renowned **Detroit Jazz Festival** during Labor Day weekend. A lively mood is produced by the music as it reverberates through the city's streets.

Join the tradition of viewing **America's Thanksgiving Parade** on Thanksgiving Day, a renowned event that includes ornate floats, marching bands, and Santa Claus himself.

Dally in the Alley (September): This Midtown Detroit arts and music event honors the inventiveness of the community. A vibrant and diverse ambiance is created by the gathering of local musicians, artists, and food sellers.

These are just a handful of the occasions that make Detroit vibrant all year long. Organizing your vacation around one of these events might give your trip a special and unforgettable touch.

Consider your choices for the weather, activities, and cultural experiences as you prepare to go to Detroit. Every season has something unique to offer, and the city's festivals give you a chance to fully experience its vivacious energy. Therefore, Detroit is prepared to greet you with open arms whether you're attracted to the springtime blooms or the holiday lights.

TRAVEL ESSENTIALS

To guarantee a seamless and pleasurable journey, planning for your trip to Detroit requires addressing several important travel necessities. The **"Detroit Travel Guide 2023"** will walk you through significant factors in this part.

Visa and Entry Requirements

Understand the visa and entrance procedures for your trip to Detroit before you pack your luggage, especially if you're coming from overseas. What you need to know is as follows:

Visa Requirements: Many nations' nationals must get a visa to enter the United States. To find out whether you need a visa, check the website of the U.S. Department of State or get in touch with the American embassy or consulate in your area.

The Visa Waiver Program (**VWP**) may make it possible for citizens of visa-exempt nations (such as the majority of European nations) to travel to the United States without a visa. You must apply for an Electronic System for Travel Authorization (ESTA) online before your travel to do this.

Validity of Passport: Ensure that your passport is valid for at least six months after the date on which you want to exit the United States.

Customs and Declarations: Become familiar with U.S. customs laws and the products you are permitted to and are not permitted to import. On your customs declaration form, be honest.

Transportation

Thanks to a multitude of transit alternatives, getting about Detroit is quite simple:

If you're traveling into Detroit, you'll probably land at DTW **(Detroit Metropolitan Wayne County Airport).** With many terminals, it is one of the busiest airports in the United States. Taxis, ride-sharing services, airport shuttles, and rental vehicles may all take you from the airport to the city center.

Public Transportation: The Detroit Department of Transportation (DDOT) and the Suburban Mobility Authority for Regional Transportation (SMART) run the city's public transportation system. Within the city, buses are a widely used form of transportation.

Ridesharing: In Detroit, businesses like Uber and Lyft provide easy and effective transportation across the city.

Renting a vehicle is a practical choice if you want to visit locations outside of Detroit. Rental companies are accessible around the city and at the airport.

Biking: Thanks to designated bike lanes and bike-sharing systems like MoGo, Detroit has grown more bicycle-friendly. Cycling across the city is a fun and environmentally responsible activity.

Accommodations

To accommodate a variety of interests and budgets, Detroit has a broad selection of lodging options:

Hotels: There are several hotels in Downtown Detroit, including upscale establishments like The Shinola Hotel and revered landmarks like the Detroit Foundation Hotel. Boutique hotels are also available in Midtown and Corktown, while well-known brand hotels may be found on the outskirts.

Bed & Breakfasts: In some of Detroit's historic districts, take in the elegance of a bed and breakfast. are warmly furnished with a distinctive touch.

Throughout the city, several Airbnb listings provide visitors the chance to stay in distinctive homes such as lofts in old industrial structures or chic flats.

Hostels: If you're on a tight budget, think about booking a room at one of Detroit's hostels, which provide reasonably priced housing in dorms.

lengthier Stay: For lengthier stays, extended stay hotels or serviced apartments provide a cozy, kitchen-equipped environment.

Consider location, facilities, and ratings when making a reservation to choose the place that best matches your requirements. Always make reservations well in advance, particularly during busy travel times or during significant events.

Packing Tips

Effective packing may improve your trip to Detroit and make sure you're ready for a variety of activities and weather conditions:

Dress appropriately for the weather based on the time of year you will be visiting. Winters call for warm layers, while summers may call for light attire. For city exploration, don't forget a pair of suitable walking shoes.

Equipment and Adapters: Bring your smartphone, camera, and chargers, as well as any other necessary equipment. If your gadgets need a different plug type or voltage range than what is used in the United States (Type A or Type B outlets), you may need a plug adapter or voltage converter.

Travel documents: Store your passport, visa, travel insurance, and other crucial papers in a safe location that is also simple to find. These records should be duplicated and then kept in separate storage.

Medication: If you use prescription drugs, make sure you have enough on hand to last the whole trip. It's a good idea to have a modest first-aid kit on hand in case of minor accidents.

Travel necessities include things like a portable phone charger, sunscreen, a reusable water bottle, and a travel-sized toiletries kit.

Have some **local currency** on hand for modest purchases, but think about using credit or debit cards for most purchases. To prevent card problems, let your bank know about your vacation intentions.

You can ensure that you are well-prepared for your Detroit excursion by taking care of these travel necessities. Whether you're a first-time visitor or coming back to see more, Detroit's friendly environment and variety of attractions are waiting to be discovered.

EXPLORING DETROIT

Detroit is a vibrant city with a rich tapestry of history and culture. You must see the city's numerous areas and sites to fully understand its character. We explore Downtown Detroit in this part since it is the city's beating heart.

Detroit's downtown

Downtown Detroit is the city's resurgence hub; here, modernity and history collide and a tangible energy penetrates the streets. Anyone touring the Motor City must go there.

Campus Martius Park

Campus Martius Park is a hive of activity all year long and is often referred to be the "**point of origin**" for Detroit. Detroiters congregate there to celebrate, unwind, and network. Here's what to anticipate:

Campus Martius' Beach: In the summer, the park is transformed into a city beach with sand, deck chairs, and a beach bar. It's the ideal location for relaxing in the sun and sipping a cool beverage.

Winter Magic: During the winter months, Campus Martius is transformed into a winter paradise with the biggest ice skating rink in the city, which is encircled by sparkling lights and a grand Christmas tree. The Christmas celebrations in Detroit are centered there.

Live Music and Events: Throughout the year, the park offers free performances, movie evenings, and cultural gatherings. To find out what's happening during your visit, look at the event calendar.

Food Truck Fridays: Throughout the warmer months, food trucks congregate in the park on Fridays to provide a wide variety of delectable dishes. A foodie's fantasy has come true.

There are several eating alternatives around Campus Martius, ranging from fine dining establishments to fast food joints, so you're never far from a great lunch.

Riverfront in Detroit

The Detroit River shoreline is one of the city's most alluring characteristics. A beautiful area to visit, the Detroit Riverfront has experienced a remarkable makeover in recent years.

The Ambassador Bridge to Canada and the Detroit skyline are both visible from the Riverwalk, a beautiful route that runs beside the river. It's ideal for a calm jog, bike ride, or leisurely walk.

Outdoor Activities: The Riverfront is peppered with parks and green areas that beckon guests to unwind, have a picnic, or engage in outdoor activities. Kayaks and paddleboards may also be rented to get a different view of the city.

Explore sites like the **William G. Milliken State Park** and **Harbor at the Rivard Plaza**, or go to the Detroit RiverFront Conservancy for details on future events and activities.

Dining with a View: There are several waterfront eateries and pubs that provide breathtaking views of the river and cityscape. Take in the natural beauty while eating or drinking.

Historic Buildings

Historic buildings in Downtown Detroit are a treasure mine, representing the glorious history of the area. Here are some famous structures you shouldn't pass up:

The Guardian Building, a National Historic Landmark and "Cathedral of Finance," is a magnificent example of Art Deco design. Enter to see its magnificent interior, which showcases colorful mosaics and elaborate details.

The Fisher Building is another masterpiece of Art Deco and a testimony to luxury. Admire the lobby's marble finish and the "Theater Building" next door, which houses the Fisher Theatre, a popular venue for Broadway performances.

Penobscot Building: This skyscraper is a masterpiece of Art Deco and is recognized for its eye-catching spire. It continues to be an architectural masterpiece despite formerly being Detroit's tallest structure.

Experience the **grandeur of the Fox Theatre**, a gorgeously restored cinema palace from the 1920s that today plays home to Broadway performances, concerts, and other events. A stunning fusion of Persian, Indian, and Asian patterns may be seen within.

A Detroit landmark, The Renaissance Center (GM Renaissance Center) is made up of seven linked buildings. Although it is mostly used as General Motors' corporate offices, you may tour its lower floors to see the Detroit Riverfront, shops, and restaurants.

These historical structures provide a window into the city's economic and cultural past in addition to serving as a display of Detroit's talent in architecture. During your stay, be sure to find out whether any of these attractions offer guided tours.

Discovering Downtown Detroit is a fascinating trip through the city's past, present, and dynamic future. Downtown Detroit provides a wide variety of experiences that will leave you with enduring memories of this magnificent city, from the urban beach of Campus Martius Park to the scenic Riverwalk and the grandeur of historic structures. Downtown Detroit offers plenty to offer any tourist, whether they are history buffs, nature lovers, or just searching for a taste of city life.

MIDTOWN AND CULTURAL CENTER

Midtown Detroit and the Cultural Center are thriving communities that hum with education, art, and culture. It's like taking a trip through Detroit's creative essence to explore this neighborhood.

Detroit Institute of Arts

The Detroit Institute of Arts, often known as the DIA, is an important part of the city's aesthetic character and a cultural treasure trove. Here is what to anticipate when you go:

World-class Art Collection: The DIA is home to more than 65,000 pieces of artwork from different eras and regions. The collection is a tribute to human inventiveness, ranging from ancient

Egyptian mummies to European masterpieces by painters like Van Gogh and Rembrandt.

The set of frescoes by famous Mexican artist Diego Rivera is one of the DIA's most recognizable elements. They are known as the "Detroit Industry Murals." These murals, which portray the industrial history of the city, are a must-see since they provide light on Detroit's past.

Special exhibits: The DIA presents transient exhibits that highlight various artistic mediums and subjects. For the most recent exhibits while you are there, check the museum website.

Family-friendly Programs: The DIA provides events and activities for people of all ages, including galleries that are interactive for kids and families. Everyone may experience art there as it comes to life.

The Detroit Film Theatre, which shows independent, international, and vintage movies in a gorgeously renovated old theater, is a must-see for cinephiles.

Museum of African American History

A tribute to the African American experience and contributions to the cultural fabric of the city is Detroit's Museum of African American History. This is what you'll discover:

A Journey Through History: View displays that trace the development and accomplishments of African Americans in Detroit, from slavery through the Civil Rights Movement and beyond.

For individuals with a passion for African-American history and genealogy, the Charles H. Wright Library is an invaluable resource.

It has a sizable collection of books, papers, and manuscripts.

Oral history project: The museum's oral history project archives the voices and narratives of African Americans in Detroit and offers a close-up and personal view of the history of the area.

Educational Programs: To promote a greater knowledge of African-American history and culture, the museum conducts educational programs and seminars for students as well as the general public.

Detroit Science Center

Visitors of all ages will love the Detroit Science Center because it is a place where curiosity knows no boundaries. This is what you can look into:

Interactive Exhibits: The Science Center offers hands-on displays on a variety of subjects, including biology, geology, physics, and astronomy. Visitors may learn and explore with their hands.

IMAX cinema: In the Science Center's IMAX cinema, discover the marvels of the natural world and space as larger-than-life movies transport you on magnificent expeditions.

Planetarium: Take a trip across space in the planetarium at the Science Center. Immersive displays that attract both children and adults let viewers explore the stars, planets, and galaxies.

Programs for Education: The Science Center offers seminars and programs for education that are geared at families and school groups, encouraging STEM (Science, Technology, Engineering, and Mathematics) study in a fun manner.

Check the Science Center's schedule for unique events, such as exhibitions and activities with a scientific theme that provides a deeper look into certain scientific subjects.

Midtown Detroit and the **Cultural Center** are important centers for learning, the arts, and culture. They provide a wide variety of activities that showcase the city's innovative spirit and dedication to education. The DIA's world-class artwork, the Science Center's pique your interest, or the DIA's exploration of African American history all promise to deepen your awareness of Detroit's cultural diversity. They serve as evidence of the city's unwavering commitment to promoting innovation, education, and exploration.

EASTERN MARKET AND CORKTOWN

Any traveler must stop in at Eastern Market and Corktown, two Detroit districts that provide a unique combination of gastronomic treats and vintage charm.

Exploring the Markets

One of the biggest historic public marketplaces in the United States, Eastern Market is a foodie's heaven. Here are some things to anticipate:

Fresh fruit, artisanal cheeses, baked goods, flowers, and other items are all sold at the market's vibrant Saturday farmers' market. It's a busy, vibrant setting that captures the essence of Detroit's culinary sector.

Specialized food merchants: Throughout the week, the market is home to specialized food merchants that sell anything from gourmet meats and seafood to spices and imported ingredients. It's an excellent location for finding unusual foods and culinary ideas.

Beyond food, Eastern Market sells the goods of regional artists and craftspeople. You may buy handcrafted jewelry, original paintings, and mementos with Detroit themes.

Community Feeling: There is a strong feeling of belonging at the market. Locals and visitors mix, and there is a warm and inviting environment. Live music and food trucks often enhance the celebratory atmosphere.

One of Detroit's oldest districts, Corktown is close to Eastern Market and has a colorful past. What makes it unique is as follows:

Historic Sites in Corktown

This renowned railroad station, which was long deserted, is receiving a significant refurbishment. The building's outside is magnificent and represents Detroit's resiliency even though you can't enter it yet.

Tiger Stadium Site: A community baseball diamond currently stands where the legendary Tiger Stadium once stood. The pitcher's mound's preservation serves as a moving reminder of the stadium's history.

Corktown is renowned for its beautifully maintained 19th-century architecture, which includes vibrant row buildings and charming streets. It's a lovely area to take a leisurely walk in.

Local Restaurants and Pubs: Corktown is home to some of Detroit's top bars and eateries, including the well-known Slows Bar BQ. It's the ideal location for enjoying a delectable lunch and discovering the city's culinary culture.

The second-oldest continually running **Catholic parish in the country is St. Anne de Detroit Catholic Church,** which was established in 1701. It is a must-see because of its magnificent architecture and historical importance.

Corktown and Eastern Market provide a great contrast in atmospheres. While Corktown welcomes you to go back in time and discover the city's historical foundations, Eastern Market immerses you in a buzzing food-focused environment. They are crucial stops for any tourist wishing to comprehend the diverse culture and history of Detroit since they together demonstrate the variety and resiliency that constitute the city's identity.

Belle Isle Park

A beautiful island haven in the Detroit River, Belle Isle Park is a natural beauty that provides a variety of outdoor activities for nature lovers and leisure seekers alike:

Belle Isle has a 5.2-mile scenic road around the island and provides breathtaking views of the river and the Detroit skyline. Scenic drives are also available, as are picnic areas. Visitors are invited to make use of the many picnic sites with BBQ grills where they may eat quietly and beautifully.

Swimming and Beaches: The island has several beaches, including the well-known Belle Isle Beach and the quiet Conservatory Beach. It's a nice place to swim, sunbathe, or enjoy a seaside picnic in the summer.

Nature paths: Belle Isle has a network of paths that are great for birding and hiking. Enjoy the island's natural splendor while exploring ponds, meadows, and forested regions.

Fishing: The island's banks of the Detroit River and its lagoons provide several options for fishing. Fish including bass, pike, and perch are often caught.

Water sports: Canoeing and kayaking are popular pursuits, and anyone wishing to paddle across the island's rivers may hire equipment. It is appropriate for all ability levels because of the calm seas.

Biking: Belle Isle is a cyclist's paradise because of its designated bike lanes and pathways. To explore the island's various attractions, either bring your bike or hire one there.

Anna Scripps Whitcomb Conservatory

A must-see site is the Anna Scripps Whitcomb Conservatory, which is located on Belle Isle and is a horticultural wonder:

Botanical Diversity: The conservatory is home to a varied variety of plants from all over the globe, including species from the tropics, the desert, and the temperate zone. In its numerous chambers, you'll discover rare orchids, tall palms, and aromatic blossoms.

Architectural Grace: The conservatory's magnificent architecture transports visitors to a bygone period of opulent conservatories with its towering glass dome and exquisite ironwork.

The Lily Pond is an idyllic location for photography and reflection outside the conservatory. It is surrounded by water lilies and koi fish.

Opportunities for Education: The conservatory provides educational classes, programs, and tours, making it a fun destination for people of all ages interested in botany and horticulture.

The Anna Scripps Whitcomb Conservatory and Belle Isle Park each have something unique to offer, whether you're looking for outdoor activities, tranquility by the lake, or the ability to immerse yourself in a world of botanical delights. It demonstrates Detroit's dedication to protecting the environment and offering recreational opportunities to locals and tourists alike.

MOTOWN MUSIC HERITAGE

The Motown Museum

The Motown Museum, often known as "**Hitsville U.S.A.**," is a revered destination for music lovers all around the globe. An immersive trip through the history of the illustrious record company is provided by this historic home, where the Motown sound was created:

The Birthplace of Hits: Berry Gordy launched Motown Records in 1959, which is where many of the most well-known songs in music history were created. Fans of soul, R&B, and pop music consider the Motown Museum, which is located in the same building where these classics were recorded, to be sacred ground.

The studio where The Supremes, Marvin Gaye, and Stevie Wonder recorded their songs is Studio A, the museum's centerpiece. It is an intense and moving experience to be there in the space where these musical luminaries produced their songs.

Artifacts and Memorabilia: The museum is a veritable gold mine of Motown artifacts, including costumes, musical equipment, and performers' personal effects. These items provide light on the personalities of the artists who defined a period.

Guided Tours: Expert guides walk guests through Motown's history while telling anecdotes and tales about the label's ascent to success. You'll get a profound respect for the creativity and brilliance that characterized Motown's heyday.

HITSVILLE U.S.A.

The initial Motown office, commonly referred to as Hitsville U.S.A., provides an insight into the label's modest beginnings:

Historical Importance: In 1959, Berry Gordy converted the home at 2648 West Grand Boulevard in Detroit into the Motown corporate headquarters. It's where the Motown family lived, worked, and produced music that has stood the test of time and cut over racial and socioeconomic barriers.

The modest recording studios were renowned for songs like "**My Girl**" by The Temptations and "Stop! In the Name of Love" by The Supremes were created and may be explored at Hitsville U.S.A. The music created here has a colossal effect in contrast to the humble surroundings.

The "**echo chamber**" in the basement, where engineers developed reverb effects for Motown songs, is one distinctive feature. It's evidence of the cutting-edge methods used to create the Motown sound.

Berry Gordy's legacy: The storyline of Hitsville includes a significant amount of information on Berry Gordy's vision, tenacity, and commitment to developing emerging talent. Here, his reputation as a music industry titan and cultural innovator is honored.

A voyage into the heart of American music history may be had by visiting the Motown Museum and Hitsville U.S.A. It is a location where the Motown magic was created and where it still finds new artists and fans to inspire. You can practically hear the echoes of the musicians that helped Motown become a worldwide phenomenon as you walk through these revered halls..

SPORTS AND ENTERTAINMENT

Catching a Tigers game

Catching a Detroit Tigers baseball game at Comerica Park is an amazing experience for sports fans:

Baseball Tradition: The Tigers have a great baseball history that dates back to 1901, and going to a game allows you to be a part of it.

Comerica Park: With a carousel, a Ferris wheel, and a recognizable brick façade, the stadium is a wonder in and of itself. Both before and during the game, you may explore the park's distinctive features.

Feel the energy of the crowd as you join other supporters in supporting the Tigers. The atmosphere at the stadium is tremendous, particularly when the game is tight.

Comerica Park provides a wide variety of food choices, ranging from traditional hot dogs and peanuts to gourmet cuisine. A local favorite, the Detroit coney dog, should not be missed.

Family-Friendly: Tigers games are kid-friendly, with special play areas and a Ferris wheel that offers breathtaking stadium views.

Entertainment Districts

There are several entertainment areas in Detroit where you may relax and take in the city's nightlife:

Downtown Entertainment: There are pubs, clubs, and music venues in Downtown Detroit to satisfy every taste. After dark, the area comes alive with live music, DJs, and dance floors for those who want to party all night long.

Greektown is renowned for its energetic environment and is home to a large number of eateries, pubs, and the Greektown Casino. You may enjoy Mediterranean food there and try your luck at the slots.

Midtown's Cultural Scene: With theaters, art galleries, and music venues that appeal to a more educated clientele, Midtown provides a unique kind of nightlife. For those seeking an elegant evening of entertainment, this area is ideal.

Corktown's Hip Hangouts: The historic neighborhood of Corktown is home to hip bars and pubs that draw a variety of patrons. Enjoy live music, handmade beverages, and the companionship of locals and other tourists.

Casinos: The MGM Grand Detroit and MotorCity Casino Hotel are only two of the casinos in Detroit. These places provide a variety of entertainment alternatives, whether you like gaming or are simply seeking for a fun setting.

The sports and entertainment culture of Detroit is proof of its tenacity and inventiveness. The city understands how to keep tourists amused and involved, from the boom of the fans at a Tigers game to the vibrant nightlife in its entertainment areas. If you like sports, and music, or are just looking for a great night out, Detroit has something to offer you.

BEYOND DETROIT: Day Trips from Detroit

While Detroit has many attractions, traveling beyond the municipal boundaries brings up a world of interesting opportunities. The following are some amazing day excursions you may do from Detroit:

Ann Arbor

The attractive city of Ann Arbor, which is just 45 minutes west of Detroit, is well-known for its thriving arts community, sophisticated culture, and stunning natural surroundings. What to do in Ann Arbor is listed below:

University of Michigan: The esteemed University of Michigan is located in Ann Arbor. Visit the University of Michigan Museum of Art, meander across the lovely campus, and take in the college vibe.

Kerrytown: With its unique stores, art galleries, and the Ann Arbor Farmers' Market, this historic neighborhood is a creative hotspot. It's a fantastic location to discover handmade products and original presents.

The 123-acre Nichols Arboretum, sometimes known as the "Arb," is a botanical paradise with tranquil walks, luxuriant plants, and picturesque vistas of the Huron River.

Ann Arbor has a thriving culinary culture, with a wide variety of eateries, cafés, and bakeries. Be sure to check out the renowned sandwiches at Zingerman's Delicatessen and local farm-to-table fare.

Windsor, Canada

The Detroit-Windsor Tunnel and the Ambassador Bridge make it simple to travel from Detroit to Windsor, Canada. A variety of cultural events, waterfront vistas, and gastronomic treats are available in Windsor:

Caesars Windsor: If you're feeling fortunate, you may enjoy live entertainment, food choices, and exciting gaming at Caesars Windsor Casino.

Walk Along the Riverfront: Take in the expansive vistas of the Detroit skyline as you stroll along the Windsor Riverfront. Even a boat excursion is available to explore the Detroit River.

Enjoy dishes from Canada, such as poutine, butter tarts, and sandwiches with peameal bacon. Due to its diversified population, Windsor is renowned for its vibrant eating scene.

History and art: Discover Canadian and Indigenous art at the Art Gallery of Windsor, or learn about the history of Canada at the Canadian Historical Museum.

Henry Ford Museum

The Henry Ford Museum and Greenfield Village in Dearborn, just outside Detroit, provide a fascinating tour through American history and innovation:

The Henry Ford Museum exhibits the advancement of American industry and innovation. There are vintage cars like the Rosa Parks bus and the Kennedy assassination limousine to be found. History comes to life with interactive exhibitions, such as the opportunity to ride in a Model T.

Greenfield Village: A living history museum with over 80 historic buildings, including the Wright

Brothers' bicycle store and Thomas Edison's Menlo Park laboratory, Greenfield Village is located next to the museum. With demonstrations and tales from various times, costumed interpreters bring history to life.

Take the Ford Rouge Factory Tour if you're captivated by the manufacturing industry. It has a catwalk above the assembly line and provides an inside view of how Ford vehicles are made today.

Benson Ford Research Center: The Benson Ford Research Center is home to a sizable collection of records, images, and artifacts about American history, invention, and technology.

These excursions from Detroit give a thorough study of the area, including cultural encounters, historical insights, and scenic beauty. Each excursion provides a distinctive viewpoint that enhances your Detroit experience, whether you decide to immerse yourself in the intellectual atmosphere of Ann Arbor, cross international boundaries to Windsor, or explore American history at the Henry Ford Museum. Don't be afraid to go beyond the municipal boundaries to find the many treasures that are waiting in the neighboring towns.

EXPLORING MICHIGAN:
Beyond Detroit

The wide and varied state of Michigan, sometimes known as the "Great Lakes State," is home to a variety of natural wonders, recreational activities, and cultural experiences. Following are a few places outside of Detroit that you must visit:

Lake Michigan Shoreline

Sand beaches, quaint communities, and breathtaking sunsets along Michigan's western coast along Lake Michigan:

Traverse City: A mecca for food and wine lovers, Traverse City is known for its cherry orchards and vineyards. Visit the Old Mission Peninsula's vineyards, savor some fresh cherries, and unwind on the city's lovely beaches.

Towering dunes, luxuriant woods, and crystal-clear seas may all be found in Sleeping Bear Dunes National Lakeshore. Take picturesque drives, hike the dunes, and stand atop the bluffs to take in the mesmerizing vistas.

Holland: Known for its Dutch roots, Holland offers calming beaches like Holland State Park, vibrant tulip festivals, and a quaint center.

Grand Haven: See the recognizable red lighthouse at Grand Haven State Park. Take a stroll along the promenade, enjoy musical fountain performances, and relax on the sandy beaches.

The Upper Peninsula

The Upper Peninsula (UP) of Michigan is a wild and rugged paradise filled with expansive woods, beautiful lakes, and outdoor activities:

Pictured Rocks National Lakeshore is recognized for its breathtaking sandstone cliffs, waterfalls, and crystal-clear waters. Pictured Rocks is situated along Lake Superior's southern coast. Awe-inspiring vistas of this natural beauty are available when hiking, kayaking, and on boat cruises.

Tahquamenon Falls State Park is a lush wilderness region ideal for hiking and camping and is home to the stunning Tahquamenon Falls. The Upper and Lower Falls are mesmerizing, particularly in the fall when they are encircled by colorful vegetation.

Copper Harbor is a peaceful retreat located at the extremity of the Keweenaw Peninsula. Take a trek up Brockway Mountain Drive, see Fort Wilkins Historic State Park, and enjoy sweeping views of Lake Superior.

This secluded island, which can only be reached by boat, is a backpacker's dream. It is a protected wilderness area, making hiking and camping there perfect. The region has beautiful lakes, lush woods, and a variety of species.

Mackinac Island

Between Michigan's Upper and Lower Peninsulas, Mackinac Island offers a glimpse into the past with its Victorian elegance and no-car zone:

The island is renowned for its maintained old buildings, which include the illustrious Grand Hotel, where visitors may relive the opulence of yore.

Cars are not permitted on the island, hence the only modes of mobility are bicycles and horse-drawn carriages. Take a leisurely carriage trip or rent a bike to explore the beautiful paths.

Shops selling fudge: Mackinac Island is well known for its fudge. For a sweet treat and to see how traditional fudge is made, stop by one of the numerous fudge shops.

Natural Beauty: The island has hiking paths, beautiful views, and chances for outdoor pursuits like horseback riding and kayaking. For those who like the outdoors, Arch Rock and Mackinac Island State Park are popular destinations.

These locations outside of Detroit highlight the variety of natural beauty and experiences Michigan has to offer. Travelers seeking adventure, leisure, and cultural immersion will find a wide variety of experiences in Michigan, from the peaceful beaches of Lake Michigan to the untamed wildness of the Upper Peninsula and the timeless appeal of Mackinac Island. Every location guarantees enduring memories and a closer connection to the state's natural and cultural heritage.

EXPERIENCING LOCAL CULTURE: Dining in Detroit

Detroit's varied population, long history, and resilient spirit are all reflected in the city's culinary sector. The city provides a mouthwatering variety of cuisines that perfectly represent the spirit of Detroit's culture, from soul food to modern cuisine. An example of things to enjoy in the Motor City is given below:

Must-Try Dishes

A beef or pork hot dog is topped with chili sauce, onions, and mustard on a steamed bun to make the Coney Dog, a Detroit institution. For centuries, two renowned cafes, American Coney Island and Lafayette Coney Island, have been dishing up these delectable dogs, igniting friendly competition over which one is the best.

Pizza made in Detroit style is a delicacy that you just must experience. The crust is thick and rectangular, crispy on the exterior and soft on the inside, and it is covered with tomato sauce and cheese, which often reaches the pan's edge to form a caramelized, cheesy crust. To enjoy this regional specialty, go to Buddy's Pizza, one of the pioneers of Detroit-style pizza.

Detroit has a strong affinity for soul food, and its cuisine is influenced by the South. At famed soul food restaurants like Kuzzo's Chicken & Waffles or Bert's Marketplace, indulge in meals like fried chicken, collard greens, macaroni and cheese, and sweet potato pie.

Paczki: You're in for a treat if you go to Detroit on Fat Tuesday, also known as Paczki Day. Polish pastries known as paczki are filled with a variety of sweet fillings, such as custard or raspberry, and then sprinkled with powdered sugar. These delicious goods are produced in large quantities by the Polish bakeries in Detroit, such as New Martha Washington Bakery.

Iconic Restaurants

Slows Bar BQ is a Corktown landmark known for its delectable BBQ. The smoked meats are tender and oozing with flavor, including pulled pork and beef brisket. Make sure to get a side of their acclaimed mac 'n cheese.

Supino Pizzeria: This Eastern Market establishment is home to some of the greatest thin-crust pizzas in the area. Each slice is a gastronomic beauty thanks to its inventive toppings, such as fig and prosciutto or roasted red pepper and feta.

Selden Standard: A farm-to-table establishment that helped establish Detroit's modern eating scene.

Seasonal ingredients are used in their constantly evolving cuisine, which is expertly and creatively prepared.

This Midtown treasure, Chartreuse Kitchen & Cocktails, mixes cutting-edge cooking with environmentally friendly methods. The menu stands out in Detroit's culinary scene because it emphasizes locally produced products and creative beverages.

Gold Cash Gold: Located in Corktown and featuring Southern-inspired food with a modern twist, Gold Cash Gold is housed in a gorgeously refurbished historic structure. The chef's inventiveness is on display in dishes like cornmeal gnocchi and buttermilk fried chicken.

Detroit is a center for **culinary innovation** in addition to being a metropolis of automotive invention. Detroit's culinary culture is as diverse as the city itself, with well-known foods like Coney Dogs and Detroit-style pizza as well as a thriving eating scene that embraces variety and creativity. Discovering regional cuisine is a great way to get to know Detroit's heart and soul, experiencing the tastes and customs that make this amazing city unique. Pull up a chair, enjoy the flavors, and join the culinary history of Detroit.

NIGHTLIFE AND ENTERTAINMENT

The nightlife and entertainment scene in Detroit is active and diverse, providing a wide range of activities for cultural vultures and night owls alike. Detroit offers something for everyone, whether you want to dance the night away or listen to live music in a cozy atmosphere.

Live Music Venues

The Fillmore Detroit is a renowned venue for live music. It is a historic theater in the heart of Detroit. Rock, pop, hip-hop, and electronic musical acts are all performed at The Fillmore, which provides an elegant but cozy atmosphere. A unique musical experience is guaranteed by the venue's elaborate decor and cutting-edge sound equipment.

Saint Andrew's Hall is a well-known Detroit music venue that is housed in a historic church. It is renowned for having great acoustics and has welcomed famous performers from many genres. The compact setting of the theater fosters a special bond between performers and spectators.

Cliff Bell's is a must-go-to if you want some jazz and elegance. This Art Deco treasure pays homage to the jazz period in Detroit and presents live jazz concerts in a seductive, refined environment. Enjoy a meal that was influenced by the city's past and handmade beverages.

El Club: El Club is a refuge for independent music with a broad roster of regional and international musicians. It's a popular hangout for music lovers wanting to discover up-and-coming acts because of its welcoming environment and diversified programming.

Clubs and bars

Deluxx Fluxx is a unique combination of an art installation and a nightclub, and it is situated in Belt Alley. Dancing to electronic rhythms takes place in an immersive setting with arcade games and colorful sights.

A refuge for gamers and retro-lovers, Ready Player One is a pub and arcade combination. It's a fun place for a night out with a wide variety of retro arcade games and themed beverages.

The Keep is a secret treasure in downtown Detroit if you like handmade drinks and speakeasy atmospheres. It's a cozy place for enjoying handcrafted cocktails, hidden away in the Marlin Building's basement.

Marble Bar: This adaptable establishment is well-known for its wide range of musical selections, which range from punk and rock to techno and house. It's a wonderful spot to mingle and take in live entertainment because of its roomy interior and rooftop terrace.

Detroit's shopping

The retail environment in Detroit is evidence of the inventiveness and originality of the city. There are many chances to explore Detroit's flair, from small stores bursting with handcrafted items to neighborhood boutiques providing one-of-a-kind fashion treasures.

Local Boutiques

Shinola is a company located in Detroit that is renowned for its well-produced watches, bicycles, leather goods, and other products. Their main location in Midtown not only exhibits their merchandise but also pays homage to the city's industrial past.

Nest: Nest is a stylish store in Eastern Market that offers a well-picked assortment of apparel, accessories, and home items. It's the ideal location to discover uncommon presents or freshen up your wardrobe with fashionable findings.

The **Peacock Room** is a vintage-inspired shop that promotes femininity and classic elegance. It is housed in the Fisher Building. A veritable gold mine of vintage and vintage-inspired apparel and accessories may be found.

Mama Coo's Boutique is a lovely store stocked with unique items that are tucked away in the center of Corktown. It's a hotspot of Detroit innovation, offering everything from antique apparel and jewelry to local artwork and home furnishings.

Souvenirs and Artisanal Goods

Detroit Mercantile Co.: This hidden treasure in Eastern Market honors Detroit's history with a collection of locally produced items, antiques, and memorabilia. It's the perfect spot to find unusual mementos.

The Detroit Artists Market, which was established in 1932, exhibits the creations of regional artists. From paintings and sculptures to jewelry and ceramics, you may discover a wide variety of artwork that lets you bring a bit of Detroit's artistic soul home.

City Bird is a charming store featuring Detroit-themed gifts and handcrafted items that are situated in the Cass Corridor. It's a one-stop shop for Detroit nostalgia, offering anything from locally created candles to stationery inspired by the city.

For fans of stationery and letterpress printing, **Signal-Return** is a hidden treasure. This locally owned letterpress workshop and print store offers exquisitely made paper items and one-of-a-kind presents.

An opportunity to bring a bit of the city's passion and workmanship home is provided by Detroit's retail scene, which promotes regional talent and ingenuity. The city's shopping attractions provide a glimpse into its rich culture and ingenuity, whether you're perusing distinctive shops for fashion discoveries, looking for one-of-a-kind trinkets, or immersing yourself in Detroit's flourishing art scene.

The distinctive character of the city and dedication to promoting regional artists and small businesses are reflected in each boutique and shop. Shop to your heart's delight and learn about Detroit's creative pulse.

FESTIVALS AND EVENTS:
Celebrating Detroit's Culture

Year-round festivals and events that highlight the city's rich history and modern creative energy serve to highlight Detroit's cultural vibrancy. These events bring together locals and tourists to celebrate excellence in music, art, innovation, and automobiles.

Detroit Jazz Festival

Over more than 40 years, the Labor Day weekend tradition of the Detroit Jazz Festival has enthralled music lovers. One of the biggest and most renowned jazz festivals in the world, this free event is hosted in the center of Detroit. Here are some reasons you should go:

I) **Jazz of the highest caliber:** The festival presents an exceptional roster of internationally famous jazz artists, representing a range of genres and decades. The concerts are a seamless fusion of history and creativity, including both established jazz greats and up-and-coming artists.

II) **Beautiful Riverfront**: The event is held at Campus Martius Park and Hart Plaza, which provide a beautiful background along the Detroit River. The beautiful city skyline and the music combine to create a memorable ambiance for attendees.

III) **The festival features workshops**, panel discussions, and instructional events in addition to concerts, making it a great place for jazz enthusiasts and newcomers to the music to visit.

All ages are catered to during the Detroit Jazz Festival, which is a family-friendly occasion. The KidBop section provides kids with engaging musical experiences, preserving the love of jazz for future generations.

Movement Electronic Music Festival

Every Memorial Day weekend, thousands of electronic music fans go to Detroit for the Movement Electronic Music Festival, a well-known occasion. It's a celebration of where techno music originated and how it became a worldwide sensation.

Techno Legends: Movement features an outstanding array of early electronic music and techno performers that take the stage on several stages. Participants may fully immerse themselves in the electronic music tradition of Detroit.

Underground Feeling: The movement celebrates modern, underground electronic music while also honoring the legacy of the genre. It provides a stage for up-and-coming artists to demonstrate their originality and inventiveness.

Techno Talks: The movement includes panel talks, seminars, and technological demonstrations in addition to music. It is an educational experience since these workshops explore the creativity and technology underlying electronic music.

Detroit is known as the "**City of Techno**," and this is visible throughout the event. In the clubs, after-parties, and the Techno Museum, which honors the genre's pioneers, visitors may sense the city's techno energy.

North American International Auto Show

The North American International Auto Show (NAIAS) is a celebrated occasion that honors Detroit's history as the world's automotive capital.

It's an exhibition of automobile innovation and design, held every January:

World Premieres: The NAIAS is where manufacturers present their most recent products, such as concept automobiles, electric cars, and ground-breaking innovations. It is where the car industry's future is made known.

Automotive History: The program includes a look back at the development of the auto industry via the use of vintage vehicles and exhibitions. It demonstrates Detroit's ongoing influence on mobility.

Industry networking: The NAIAS brings together experts, creators, and fans from all over the globe in the automobile industry. It serves as a center for networking, teamwork, and conversations regarding the direction of transportation.

Charity Preview: Before the grand opening, a fundraising event called the Charity Preview is conducted to benefit children's charities in the area. It mixes charitable giving with an early peek at the newest car models.

The continuing vitality, inventiveness, and cultural diversity of Detroit are shown through these festivals and events. No matter whether you're a fan of jazz, electronic music, or cars, Detroit's festivals provide unique opportunities to explore the history, present, and future of the city.

They foster creativity, unite disparate groups, and honor the city's unflappable spirit. So take part in the celebrations, acquaint yourself with the local culture, and find out why Detroiters and tourists alike love the city's festivals.

Practical Information

Like any large city, Detroit has a variety of things to offer, so when visiting the city, it's important to be aware and cautious. To guarantee a secure visit, consider the following safety advice:

Staying Safe in Detroit

Be Conscious of Your Environment: Keep vigilance and awareness of your surroundings, particularly in strange places. Tourists may feel comfortable in Detroit, but it's important to use caution, especially in less popular areas.

When it's practicable, travel in groups since there is safety in numbers. Avoid going for a solo nighttime stroll in empty regions.

Use Reputable Transportation: Particularly when going out at night, stick to well-known modes of transportation like taxis, rideshares, or public transportation.

Protect Your Valuables: Keep your possessions safe, and stay away from flashing pricey accessories like jewelry or gadgets. Passports and valuables should be stored in hotel safes.

Follow Local Advice: If you have any questions about a location's safety, speak to locals or the employees at your hotel for advice.

Keep to Well-Lit Areas: When walking at night, stay on well-lit streets and steer clear of any dark lanes or shortcuts.

Emergency Contacts

Knowing who to call in an emergency is essential for your safety:

Police: To contact the police in an emergency, call 911.

Medical Emergencies: To request an ambulance in case of a medical emergency, contact 911.

Fire Department: To contact the fire department in the case of a fire, phone 911.

Non-Emergency Police: You may call the non-emergency number of your local police department for non-emergency police help or information.

Local Transportation

Getting about Detroit is rather simple, and there are several transportation choices to fit your requirements and preferences:

Public Transit

The city's bus system is managed by the Detroit Department of Transportation (DDOT), which offers thorough coverage across Detroit and connections to other suburbs. It's an accessible and inexpensive method to learn about the city.

Subway/People Mover: The elevated automated light rail system that circles downtown Detroit is called the People Mover. Although it only makes a few stops, it is useful for getting around the main sights in the city.

SMART Bus: Bus lines that link Detroit's suburbs with the city are run by the Suburban Mobility Authority for Regional Transportation (SMART). It's a practical choice for getting to locations outside of the city core.

QLine: The QLine is a cutting-edge streetcar system that connects Midtown with the city center of Detroit along Woodward Avenue. It's a productive approach to tour these thriving areas.

Rental Cars

It makes sense to rent a vehicle in Detroit if you want to see the larger metro region or go on day excursions to surrounding sites. Here are some important things to think about:

Car rental companies are present at Detroit Metropolitan Wayne County Airport (DTW), making it simple to pick up a rental car after arriving. Additionally, rental offices may be found all around the city.

Parking: There are several places to park in Detroit, including lots, garages, and on-street parking. To avoid penalties, pay attention to parking restrictions.

Traffic: Although there may be delays during rush hours, Detroit's road system is typically well-kept and simple to use. Plan your trips and, if required, utilize GPS navigation.

Biking in Detroit

As a result of its dedicated bike lanes, greenways, and bike-sharing programs, Detroit is becoming a more bicycle-friendly city. What you should know if you're thinking of bicycling in the city is as follows:

Renting a bike is simple thanks to the city of Detroit's several bike rental programs, which you may use for either quick trips or more in-depth research.

Bike Lanes: The growing network of bike lanes and trails in Detroit makes it safer and more convenient for cyclists to move about the city. Maps or applications for your area should provide defined bike paths.

Use the proper safety equipment and always wear a helmet while motorcycling. By wearing reflective material and wearing lights, you may be seen, particularly at night.

Lock Your Bike: When parking your bike, secure it with a strong lock. Bike racks are available in a lot of establishments and tourist destinations.

Respect Traffic Regulations: Since bicycles are regarded as vehicles in Detroit, riders are required to abide by all traffic regulations, such as stop signs and traffic signals.

You may have a safe and easy trip to Detroit by being prepared, taking safety measures, and using the city's transit choices. Detroit provides a rich tapestry of experiences for tourists to explore and enjoy, whether they are seeing the city's cultural sites, eating in one of the many restaurants, or taking part in one of its famed festivals.

Money and Budgeting

To guarantee a simple and hassle-free experience managing your funds when visiting Detroit, it's crucial to be aware of the local currency and banking options:

The United States Dollar **(USD)** is the unit of exchange in Detroit and the rest of the United States. The different denominations of banknotes are $1, $5, $10, $20, $50, and $100 bills. Pennies (1 cent), nickels (5 cents), dimes (10 cents), and quarters (25 cents) are the different types of coins.

Banking Hours: Banks in Detroit normally are open from 9:00 AM to 5:00 PM, Monday through Friday. A few branches may also be open on Saturdays, however, these hours may be restricted. Automated Teller Machines (ATMs) are widely dispersed and open twenty-four hours a day for financial transactions.

Although the U.S. dollar is the most widely used currency, certain exchange offices and big banks could provide currency exchange services to tourists from other countries. For the best exchange rates, it is advised to convert money before traveling to Detroit or to utilize ATMs to obtain cash in US dollars.

Credit and debit cards are accepted almost everywhere in Detroit, including at lodging facilities, eateries, retail establishments, and the majority of other establishments. The most widely used card networks are Visa, MasterCard, American Express, and Discover. To prevent any possible card problems, be sure to let your bank or credit card provider know about your vacation intentions.

ATMs: Banks, convenience shops, and other public places all have ATMs, which are widely available in Detroit. Be aware of any possible costs while using ATMs, particularly if you're using an out-of-network machine. Ask your bank if there are any partnerships or fee-free ATM solutions available in Detroit.

Budgeting Tips

In Detroit, it is both possible and enjoyable to travel on a budget. You can take advantage of the city's attractions, eating opportunities, and entertainment without going over budget by making smart travel arrangements. Here are some financial advice for your trip to Detroit:

Accommodations: Take into account staying in inexpensive lodgings like hotels, guesthouses, or hostels. Instead, look into vacation rental possibilities for affordable lodging, particularly if you're going in a group.

Public transit: The QLine streetcar and buses are only two of Detroit's reasonably priced public transportation options. You may cut your transit expenditures by buying day or weekly passes.

Eating: Enjoy Detroit's delectable cuisine without going overboard by eating at neighborhood restaurants, food trucks, and diners. In areas like Corktown and Eastern Market, look for daily promotions, happy hour discounts, and affordable eateries.

Free Attractions: There are a lot of free places to go in Detroit, including a lot of museums and art galleries. Don't miss the Detroit Institute of Arts, which welcomes residents of Wayne, Oakland, and Macomb counties for free entry to its world-class collection.

Discount Cards: City pass cards or tourist discount cards, which provide entry to several attractions at a discounted rate, can be worth buying. These cards can be an affordable way to learn about Detroit's highlights.

Enjoy the parks and outdoor areas of the city for free or at a low cost while exploring outside. For instance, Belle Isle Park provides a variety of outdoor activities such as swimming, hiking, and picnics.

The best way to take advantage of discounts, early-bird offers, and online bargains for sites, excursions, and events is to prepare ahead by doing your research and creating your schedule in advance.

Local Markets: For reasonably priced fresh vegetables, handcrafted products, and one-of-a-kind souvenirs, check out local markets

DETROIT TRAVEL GUIDE 2023

like Eastern Market. With fresh ingredients, you may make inexpensive meals.

Utilize Local Knowledge: Consult locals for advice, bargains, and insider information. Locals often have insider knowledge of the most affordable locations to dine, buy, and explore.

Budgeting applications: Use budgeting applications to keep track of your spending and establish spending limits for different categories to help you manage your money while traveling.

Detroit may be a reasonably priced travel destination that provides a wide selection of activities with careful preparation and little study. Your trip to Detroit will be pleasurable and cost-effective if you manage your money well and take advantage of all the city has to offer.

LANGUAGE AND COMMUNICATION

Although English is the main language spoken in Detroit, you could run across some other dialects and local slang. To communicate effectively during your visit, consider the following frequent words and advice:

a) **Greetings**: A simple "Hello" or "Hi" is sufficient when meeting someone. You may add "How are you?" to your welcome out of politeness. In response, say "I'm good, thank you" or "Not too bad."

b) I'm grateful. Being grateful must be expressed. Say "**Thank you**" or "**Thanks**" to someone when they assist you or do a service. Say "Thank you very much" if you wish to seem more official.

c) When requesting anything or asking for something, it's polite to use the word "**please**." Let's use the phrase "Can I have a menu, please?"

d) Saying "**Excuse me**" is polite when you need to attract someone's attention or move through a busy location.

e) Saying "**Sorry**" or "I'm sorry" when you accidentally run into someone or make a mistake demonstrates civility and regret.

f) Use "**Yes**" and "**No**" to agree or affirm and "Disagree" or "Reject" respectively. You may also use "Yeah" in place of a standard "Yes."

g) You may ask for directions by using the phrase "**Can you help me find [place]?**" or "**How can I get to [location]?**"

h) Learn how to use numbers to talk about quantities and costs. Knowing the digits for addresses and phone numbers is also helpful.

i) **Currency**: Be familiar with expressions like "Dollar," "Cents," and "Change."

j) Phrases like "I'd like to order [dish]," "Can I have the check, please?" and "Is gratuity included?" might be useful while ordering food at a restaurant.

Wi-Fi and Internet Access

For communication, navigation, and information access, you must maintain a connection while visiting Detroit. Here's how to locate Wi-Fi and make sure you have access to the internet:

Hotels: The majority of hotels in Detroit provide their visitors with free WiFi access. When checking in, be sure to inquire about Wi-Fi connectivity;

they will provide you with the network name and password.

Coffee Shops & Cafes: Customers may get free Wi-Fi at several cafes and coffee shops in Detroit. Local coffee shops and well-known brands like Starbucks often provide this service.

Restaurants: A few eateries provide free Wi-Fi, particularly those in the downtown area. Asking the employees whether there is an internet connection is a smart idea.

Public Places: There may be free Wi-Fi accessible in certain public places, such as parks and libraries. Look for signage designating Wi-Fi areas or request the local government.

Mobile Data: Verify that your cell phone plan offers data service in the US. If necessary, you may buy a local SIM card or an international data package.

Portable Wi-Fi Devices: Before your travel, think about renting a portable Wi-Fi device (sometimes referred to as a pocket Wi-Fi or mobile hotspot). These gadgets make it simple to remain online while touring the city since they let you connect various devices to the internet.

Wi-Fi applications: To discover local Wi-Fi networks, download Wi-Fi locator applications or utilize the Wi-Fi hotspot function on your smartphone.

When connecting to public Wi-Fi networks, particularly those without passwords, use caution. When managing sensitive information, such as online banking or personal accounts, use secure networks.

You'll be prepared to speak successfully and maintain contact when visiting Detroit if you are acquainted with popular terms and know where to locate Wi-Fi and internet connection. These suggestions will improve your entire experience, whether you're navigating the city's streets, making restaurant reservations, or just keeping in contact with friends and family.

APPENDICES: Useful Resources

Tourist Information Centers

You may find it helpful to stop by or call tourist information offices for advice, direction, and extra resources while touring Detroit. To make your stay more enjoyable, these facilities include maps, brochures, and other information. Here are a few of Detroit's well-known tourist information offices:

The city's official tourist group, Visit Detroit, is devoted to assisting travelers in learning about the finest of Detroit. They run the GM Renaissance Center's Welcome Center for Visitors to Detroit. Maps, pamphlets, and experienced personnel who can provide suggestions and insights on Detroit's attractions, eating, and events are available here.

Address: 400 Renaissance Center, Suite 2500, GM Renaissance Center, Detroit, MI 48243

Detroit Metro Convention & Visitors Bureau: This organization is a great resource for travelers. They provide tourist information solutions, such as brochures, travel itineraries, and event details. The location of their tourist center in the middle of Detroit is ideal.

Address: Cobo Center, 1 Washington Boulevard, Detroit, Michigan, 48226

Detroit Wayne County Metropolitan Airport (DTW) The information desks at the airport are fantastic resources for travelers flying into Detroit. You can get city overviews, transit information, and maps. Both the North Terminal and the McNamara Terminal have these workstations.

Detroit Metropolitan Wayne County Airport, 1 Detroit Metropolitan Airport, Romulus, MI 48174 is the address (McNamara Terminal).

Detroit Metropolitan Wayne County Airport, 1
Detroit Metropolitan Airport, Romulus, MI 48174
is the address (North Terminal).

These visitor information centers are set up to help
you with every part of your trip to Detroit, from
making travel arrangements to giving you
up-to-date details on activities and events. To make
the most of your visit to the Motor City, don't be
reluctant to drop by or get in touch with them.

CONCLUSION

Finally, Detroit appeals as a city of dynamic contrasts, where the past and the present collide and a lively spirit flourishes. This thorough tour has shown the many sides of the Motor City, from its illustrious musical past to its famed automotive past. Remember to factor in the city's temperature as you get ready to start your Detroit excursion and immerse yourself in its rich cultural heritage.

Discover the distinct charms of diverse areas including downtown, Midtown, and Corktown. Learn about significant historical sites, top-notch museums, and a culinary sector that embraces both tradition and innovation. Using the services in your area can help you remain secure, spend money sensibly, and maintain contact. Detroit is waiting for you, eager to tell its tales and urge you to participate in its continuing story.

AVOID THESE 15 ACTIVITIES WHILE IN DETROIT

While Detroit has a lot to offer in terms of experiences, there are several things to steer clear of to have a safe and pleasurable trip. Following are 15 activities to avoid when visiting the Motor City:

Avoiding areas: Refrain from entering strange areas, particularly at night. Keep to well-traveled areas, and ask residents or the employees at your hotel for advice.

Neglecting Safety: While Detroit is typically safe for visitors, it's important to exercise caution. Avoid leaving valuables in your vehicle unattended, and use caution in less-trafficked locations.

Ignoring Local Advice: Ignoring locals' advice on safety or areas to avoid might result in unneeded hazards.

Driving Without Insurance: If you want to hire a vehicle, be sure your insurance is sufficient. If you don't have the right insurance, you risk paying a high price in accidents.

Ignoring Parking Rules: To prevent receiving a parking citation or having your car towed, pay attention to the parking signs and rules. Detroit strictly enforces parking regulations.

Disregarding Public Transit: Take use of Detroit's public transportation choices. Public transit options include buses, the People Mover, and the QLine.

Ignoring Cultural Sensitivity: Show cultural sensitivity and courtesy for regional traditions and customs. Avoid making unfounded or insulting assumptions.

Wastefulness: Detroit supports sustainability; refrain from producing excessive garbage and leaving litter. Consider eco-friendly procedures and properly dispose of your rubbish.

Not Trying Local Cuisine: It would be a mistake to overlook Detroit's culinary industry. Try well-known foods like Coney Dogs and Detroit-style pizza instead of just eating fast food.

Avoiding Cultural Institutions: Detroit is home to several top-notch museums and galleries; don't let this opportunity to broaden your horizons pass you by.

Avoiding Locals: Interacting with locals may improve your experience. Engage in discussion, seek out advice, and discover the city from people who are most familiar with it.

Neglecting Safety Precautions: Always buckle up while driving or riding in a vehicle, and follow the rules of the road. Traffic laws are strictly enforced in Detroit.

Neglecting Outdoor Etiquette: When enjoying parks and outdoor areas, be mindful of your surroundings and other guests. Avoid leaving trash behind.

Avoiding entertainment areas: Exercise caution, but don't completely shun entertainment districts. When used appropriately, the nightlife in Downtown Detroit is bustling.

Ignoring Local Events: Detroit organizes several festivals and events; take advantage of the opportunity to participate in the city's cultural festivities.

You can ensure a secure, courteous, and fulfilling vacation to Detroit and make the most of all the city has to offer by keeping an eye out for these 15 things to stay away from.

(HAPPY TRAVELS)

Made in the USA
Las Vegas, NV
03 December 2024

13305375R00066